Spirituality in Knitting
SereKNITy dot calm

Lisbeth Duncan

FriesenPress

Suite 300 - 990 Fort St
Victoria, BC, V8V 3K2
Canada

www.friesenpress.com

Zondervan Publishing House
Grand Rapids, Michigan 49530

ISBN
978-1-03-910763-2 (Hardcover)
978-1-03-910762-5 (Paperback)
978-1-03-910764-9 (eBook)

1. CRAFTS & HOBBIES, NEEDLEWORK, KNITTING

Distributed to the trade by The Ingram Book Company

God waits for us in the inner sanctuary of the soul.

In the busyness of today's world, why do we find it so difficult to centre ourselves and acknowledge the presence of God?

Yes, there are important tasks to be done and equally important decisions to be made as we follow our daily routine.

Yes, we fall into regular habits that become time-consuming. Yet, time is the most important element we have and time that is used can never be reclaimed. We can, no matter how busy we are, find that small slot in time to meet with God.

God waits for us in the inner sanctuary of our soul. He is a very patient God but is always at work in us.

Do you ever have the strong urge to stop what you are doing? The urge to pay attention—to be still? That is God waiting for you to just be. This feeling is easy to ignore and is often not recognizable when we're consumed in our routines until that precious window of time is gone.

I have found that time as I knit. I have given myself permission to centre myself in prayer; to allow God to manage my restless spirit that is always on the move. Hermann Hesse wrote "Within you there is a stillness and a sanctuary to which you can retreat at any time and be yourself."

Using knitting, or any other handcraft as a way into contemplative prayer is not new. The Desert Fathers were fourth-century Christian hermits who chose a solitary life of prayer in the desert of Egypt. This was to devote themselves fully to union with God, but the body is naturally restless. To settle themselves and be calm, the Fathers learned to weave baskets.

* * *

Creating something with your hands helps to settle the mind and spirit into a tranquil peace. The process of basket weaving meant the most to these monks and they often destroyed the baskets when they were finished.

Learning any new craft takes an all-absorbing attention as the brain begins to adapt to new movements where the mind experiences a new kind of presence. Knitting, as the craft of choice for me, provides enrichment in my life in times of trial, of healing, of joy, and of living through other individuals' experiences.

Accompany me on this journey of spiritual reflection as we use
our love of knitting and God's word to lead us.

One

Psalm 139: 13 - 14

"For it was you who formed my inward parts;
you knit me together in my mother's womb.
I praise you, for I am fearfully and wonderfully made". (NRSV)

God knit me in my mother's womb! Such an appropriate choice of words for those of us who are so familiar with this craft.

Throughout generations in my family, of Scottish background, knitting has been a way of life. Both grandmothers always had some project on their needles: making new sweaters for each child for the winter or replacing worn cuffs on last year's well-worn sweaters. We children never knew what it was like to have store-bought socks or gloves as there was a continuous supply of them in our households; most of our socks required mending to make them last long into the winter. Pure wool was the yarn available back then, so knitted clothing was always warm. Without washing machines, all items were carefully hand-washed to prevent shrinkage and were dried equally carefully on an outside line or on the inside pulley.

In those days, keeping a smooth-running family unit was a full-time occupation and many mothers could not work outside of the home, although there were always exceptions. My maternal grandmother was on call for the local cattle market. On Mondays, while the cattle waited for their transfer of ownership, they required milking to relieve the discomfort of a full udder. Naturally, between the times for milking each cow, my grandmother had her knitting in her basket and was able to accomplish a few rows at a time; always coming closer to the end of yet another project.

I have been knitting since I was six years old. My mother taught me the two basic stitches on four needles. Knit (K)2, Purl (P)2 for three inches forming the ribbed cuff of a pair of socks for my father.

In the late 1940s, my dad had undergone abdominal surgery and was required to rest at home for some weeks. He was the only dairyman on a large milk cattle farm, so a substitute milkman was hired while he recuperated. The farmer was unable to pay both men, so he chose to pay the one who was doing the work and rightly so. Yet this left us with no income, and my mother had difficulty in providing enough food for four young children and an invalid husband. One of my uncles offered to look after him in his family home during this time, thus relieving the financial pressure. At that time, schoolchildren were encouraged to invest in a small savings programme where a half-crown a week was used to buy a stamp.

Throughout time, this mounted up and my mother cashed in some stamps as another means of supplying food for our family.

Fortunately, the farmer allowed us to buy a baker's dozen of eggs (13 instead of 12) weekly and a can of fresh milk daily.

Teaching me to knit was one of Mom's ways of coping. It was a pastime that she was familiar with and which she enjoyed immensely. For me, this new hobby occupied my six-year-old mind while awaiting the arrival home of my dad, by which time his socks were finished.

Knitting is not a spectator sport. I was not content to observe while my mom was knitting the annual supply of sleeveless vests for my three brothers and doing the absorbing task of mending cuffs and sock heels. Some of the clothing was passed down from one brother to the next and some had extra inches knitted to the waist or the sleeves to make them fit. For every stitch given or taken away, Mom always shared her knowledge.

"The greatest good you can do for another is not just to share your riches, but to reveal to him his own."
Benjamin Disraeli

Mom also taught me to pray at the beginning of each round of knitting. Moving the stitches was like moving prayer beads. The first round was for Dad's speedy recovery. The second was offering grateful thanks for the relatives who gave compassionate care to my dad. The third was in gratitude for not being displaced from the tied house that came with the job. Mom and I enjoyed creating other reasons for our prayers, and sometimes my younger brothers had good suggestions.

By the completion of the pair of hand-knitted socks, I had learned the importance of acknowledging the presence of God in every aspect of my life.

The stories in all our lives are rich, and this personal memory ranks high for me.

Two

John 6:35 (NRSV)

"I am the bread of life. Whoever comes to me will never be hungry, and whoever believes in me will never be thirsty."

My God-given life has been richly blessed. My childhood was uncomplicated and happy. I lived with the freedom of the countryside in a farming community. I absolutely loved school and was eager to learn something new every day. As one of my daughters frequently reminded me in her formative years, "I don't have that yearning for learning which you always talk about."

In our little corner of the world, we were protected from world violence as we had just come through, and were still building from, the Second World War. All was at peace.

My brothers and I traipsed across the fields looking for hedgehogs or for bird nests. We picked bluebells in the bluebell woods and we once stopped to watch a tiny field mouse build a nest in some long grass at the base of a hedge. Our house was 300 yards short of being allowed to ride a school bus, so we had to walk. We waved at our classmates as they drove past us every day. It rained a lot in southern Scotland, so there were many times when we would dry off by a radiator before classes began.

As children, we were thankful for the seasons and the merits that each season brought. We were constantly in awe of the many aspects of nature to which we were privy. When everything is going well in your own little world, it is not necessary to call on God to protect you and those you love. Many run-of-the-mill things are taken for granted so you forget that all good things come from God who is constantly in control.

Isaiah 58:2 tells us to "seek God day after day." For those whose lives are untouched by horror and devastation, we let this idea slip until we find it necessary to call on God. We all too often take everything for granted as life is all that it should be.

⊪ ✶ ✶

For this reason, I have a gratitude corner. One that is inside my home for the long winter months in Western Canada, and one that is outside and close to our bountiful vegetable garden. To no one's surprise, I have some knitting on the needles at these stations to practice the presence of God. It is so gratifying to appreciate so much. The rhythmic motion of my needles as the stitches move smoothly from one needle to another guides me from one grateful prayer to another. I am eternally grateful for the good health of my family and myself. I am always thankful for the roof over my head and for the food on my table. I appreciate the fellowship of my neighbours and my friends and for the gifts of vision and hearing.

These prayers of simplicity and contentment lead me to the many worldly concerns of all the innocent human beings who suffer from unimaginable injustices at the hands of others. I tend to allow these concerns to become an overwhelming burden. If these suffering people are unable to come to God, I offer my fervent prayer to intercede on their behalf. I pray that they might feel an awareness of God's presence alleviating some of their distress. In the most horrendous conditions, I "seek the Lord your God with all my heart" (Deuteronomy 4:29) and almost beseech Him to intervene. My prayer is that the least fortunate would "come to me and never go hungry, believe in me and never go thirsty."

I attended a conference of more than 600 women from all over the world. A group of beautifully strong and colourfully dressed women from Africa told us their stories of survival under unbelievably inhumane conditions. After suffering from so much, each woman had become ambassadors for causes that support the most vulnerable women and children. They ask that everyone pray in solidarity with those being persecuted at the hands of men. Despite their horrible stories, these women had faith, showed love, and were able to experience joyful moments in their lives. They were examples of fortitude to the rest of us.

Each Thursday, at some point in my day, I bring out one of my prayer shawl projects and knit furiously as I mentally suffer along with such victims. My prayer takes many forms and changes with the circumstances, and yet I also pray for the perpetrators. Sadly, these stories do not stop, and we hear of the many more injustices that occur daily to our fellow human beings.

* * *

Eleanor Roosevelt once said, "The purpose of life is to live it, to taste experience to the utmost, to reach out eagerly and without fear for newer and richer experience."

Why should there be those who are denied this?

Three

Psalm 46:10 (NRSV)

"Be still and know that I am God; I am exalted among the nations, I am exalted in the earth."

We continually multitask in this busy world of ours and we exhaust ourselves both mentally and physically. We tend to complicate matters by running ragged trying to solve our problems. Harassment, anger, and self-disgust envelop themselves around us as we wonder how we ever reached this stage. We should "stop and smell the roses," but just how do we stop long enough to smell anything? It takes time to slow down from a hectic pace and it must be a conscious choice. We need to be mature enough to make that decision.

My gratitude corner is where I pick up my knitting needles in my attempt to leave my busyness behind. I knit pneumonia prevention vests for small babies and tiny hats for premature babies in India. Stitches will always be on my needles when I pick them up to enter a rhythmic state of calmness. As I pray for each one of those tiny babies I am almost lulled into a meditative state. As I pause, I create a beautiful tone within me, moving the past day behind me as I am alone with God in the present with tomorrow yet to come.

Many Third World countries lack the very basics for existence, and I continue to be amazed at how little it takes to make an even small improvement for so many people. Babies wear so little clothing, and as the temperature drops significantly between day and night, some develop chest conditions that turn into pneumonia.

These tiny woollen vests are knitted in a ribbed fashion that allows them to stretch and fit firmly around the chest. As a prevention method, local nurses encourage mothers to use these and I have been told that these little vests have made a huge difference in the health of many tiny babies.

Similarly, the use of the preemie hats has decreased the death toll of numerous small babies as the loss of body heat takes place through the head.

* * *

At the end of the verse, which is quoted at the beginning of this chapter, God moves into the future where He "will be exalted among the nations." I like to believe that He is focussing on the little recipients of these life-saving vests and, as they return to better health, He will be exalted.

A quote from St. John of the Cross states that "Where this is no love, put love and you will find love."

Four

John 10:14 – 15 (NRSV)

*"I am the Good Shepherd. I know my own and
my own know me, just as the Father knows me and
I know the Father. And I lay down my life for the sheep."*

At a workshop that I attended, I learned to concentrate on the verbs of the scriptures while reading Biblical passages. In the above passage, all of the verbs are in present tense, indicating to me that when Jesus spoke these words over 2,000 years ago, he meant them to endure as present statements into eternity.

Being present. Being in the moment is difficult when we lead such busy lives, yet I have experienced some special 'in the moment' events that have been transformative. Most of these moments are stored in my memory bank to be drawn upon when life becomes too fast-paced.

In the Canadian Rockies, I have stood in the deep snow at the edge of an unbelievably beautiful lake, listening to the sound of silence. It was only when I heard a woodpecker tapping on a distant tree that broke this trance.

I have watched with breathless anticipation as the large round, red globe of the setting sun disappeared over the Hawaiian horizon.

I have marvelled at a vast carpet of bluebells in a Scottish wood as a nearby cuckoo heralds his approval of such beauty.

I have held my breath as I waited for the first breath of a newborn baby.

I could mention many more, but you will have your own similar memories. Remember to bring them to the forefront of your memory bank to enjoy them again and again.

When remembering those places and conditions, my heart wakes up to God's creative expression. Beauty is endless.

Rudyard Kipling wrote, "Teach us to delight in simple things."

* * *

One of the simplest projects in the world of knitting is to knit a bookmark. The first year that our knitting group made bookmarks, we gave dozens of them away as gifts to all the ladies of our church on Mother's Day. These tokens were different from the customary carnation as love was woven into every stitch. As a coincidence, more than the usual number of ladies had become widows during that year, so this small gesture was humbly appreciated. Some of these recipients joined our knitting group and have been able to leave that in-between space of dealing with the necessities of life following the death of a spouse and moving on without the legacy of guilt. They want to be themselves but are afraid to be loved and known for themselves. Like most women, it is difficult to spend time focusing attention on ourselves, to feed our souls by enjoying artistic pastimes, whatever they may be. During such times of discovering our inner selves, our breath is often taken away by a sensation of holy mystery, a spiritual truth, or a rare beauty.

There is a variety of knitting styles and patterns that come under the heading of rare beauty in my eyes, such as Fair Isle, Aran, and helix. However, entrelac captures my challenged imagination as I become awestruck at the results emerging from colour to colour. This format eluded me for so long and my prayer always seemed to ask for patience and understanding as I came upon one obstruction after another. It was so hard for me to master, but when I eventually came out of the other end and was smiling, I felt as if I "lay down my life for the sheep."

Entrelac knitting is composed of tiers of blocks that are set on their points to resemble patchwork. Life is composed of tiers of blocks set on their points, as we build upon our experiences, some of which teeter on points of precarious imbalance. Many of these occur when we make life choices. As we embark on our journey through life, there are many choices to be made and we are often indecisive. Sometimes we are offered opportunities and sometimes the choices are made for us. My faith belief indicates that God has a hand in negotiating the decision.

I would like to share the personal choices that were available to me as I was about to embark on the big wide world. I was educated in Scotland and was a successful student in fine arts. I gained immense pleasure from sketching, painting, knitting, sewing, and listening to classical music.

As I approached my final year in high school, Yves St. Laurent was beginning his empire in Paris and was recruiting girls with fine motor skills in stitching from all over Europe. I was encouraged to apply, but I did not have a great desire to enter that scene so did not follow that path.

I had years of elocution training, so I enjoyed speech, drama, and writing poetry. I wanted to put that training into practice which led me to apply to a national college of speech therapy. I failed an exam that was required to enter the college, so that choice was made for me.

At the very last minute, I made the best decision, and I entered a nurse training school. As it was late, and almost time for the new class to begin, I was offered a place if I promised to stick with the course until graduation. At that time, student nurses were required to live-in so 28 of us began an amazing three-year journey. Many years later, the 24 of us who remain keep in touch and meet from all corners of the world for reunions.

Knitting played an important part of my student nursing days as many of my colleagues were also knitters. During some night duty spells when patients were asleep, the knitting needles kept sleep from our eyes.

Success in knitting gives joy to my soul. I have used intervals of silence to pay greater attentiveness to God, who always accompanies me through rough passages.

Five

Lamentations 3:22, 23 (NRSV)

"The steadfast love of the Lord never ceases; his mercies never come to an end; they are new every morning; great is your faithfulness."

What a comfort it is to accept that the steadfast love of God never ceases, and His mercies never come to an end.

In this torn world, it is so difficult to understand what Jeremiah means as he laments the death of the king. Through his grief, he has hope.

Painful personal experiences drain hope from us and cause us extended grief. During these times in our lives, it is so important to be in communion with others as we commune with God. We find that common ground in knitting with a group of people, even if they have not experienced similar pain. We can use one of the many formal prayers as we perform the rhythmic movement of transferring stitches from one needle to another. We can personalize these prayers as we form the habit.

Buddha taught, "Do not dwell in the past; do not dream of the future. Concentrate the mind on the present moment."

The action of knitting helps me live in the moment, and one of the most beautiful ways to do that is to pray with my fingers. If I am knitting a simple pattern where I do not need to worry about counting each stitch, I can raise my eyes to look at the wonder of creation. It might be a tiny bird beginning to fly, a new bloom on a lovely flower, a colourful rainbow appearing in the sky, or a dew-laden spider web on the garden fence. However, my favourite image is of a group of raindrops that are on a polished leaf or hanging from a curved blade of grass, which resembles beads. The reason for my delight in this natural artwork invokes a memory from my childhood. I learned a poem by Henry Monro called, "Overheard on a Saltmarsh" where a goblin asks a nymph to give him her green glass beads as he loves them so. This is a special memory embedded in my repertoire. I find something so simple to be especially beautiful as it gives the eyes a place to rest.

I need to be still and pause and reflect on God's creativity. I compare this pause to a rest in music. This marks an interval of silence, of a breathing pause that allows music to resonate in beautiful harmony. We have many choices in music as we use our own personal favourites to lull us into a meditative state or to energize us into a lively interaction with God. I am led into an almost hypnotic state by the combination of a lovely picture, some light classical music, and wool running through my fingers. Listening to a Brahms lullaby while watching a baby sleep as I knit a bonnet for a premature baby. Marvel at the work of God's fingers creating the moon and the stars and wonder at His creation of humankind that He is constantly mindful of them.

Allow the world around you to speed along at its own hectic pace while you engage in inner peace for solace and sanctuary. If this means knitting a dozen little bonnets in the execution of this task, then so much the better.

Six

Isaiah 43:19 (NRSV)

*"I am about to do a new thing, now it springs forth;
do you not perceive it? I will even make a way in
the wilderness and rivers in the desert."*

Have you ever been afraid of trying something new? Downhill skiing, zip-lining, oil painting, growing vegetables, learning to play a musical instrument, or learning to knit?

Though my mother taught me how to knit, this craft was also on my elementary school curriculum. In Scotland, knitting was a way of life where everyone knew how it was done.

Earlier in my professional life, I was a British-trained qualified midwife. One of my more memorable experiences was when I was called out to a country home one evening where a young mother was about to deliver her second child. I had been called out too soon, but since I was not expecting any other calls that night, I decided to stay until the birth was over. One of my duties was to relax the mother—and there are several ways of doing such—but as she waited for the birth, her husband sat by the fire, strumming away at his guitar while humming gently. Their young son, Magnus, was familiar with the tune and began to accompany his dad on the vocals.

Her labour was progressing slowly, so I took out my knitting and ask my patient to do the same. She was one of the few individuals I had met who did not know how to knit. She was hesitant to learn. Intuitively, I began to show her the rudiments of casting on and knitting a few rows of plain stitches. Within a short time, she had grasped the concept and had a few inches of a tiny white baby blanket growing from her needles.

During this time, her labour was progressing quietly in the background until she announced that her time to deliver was close. After getting her into a relatively comfortable position, a healthy baby girl was safely delivered into the world.

* * *

"Behold I do a new thing; now it shall spring forth."

By focussing on repetitive action, like knitting, anxiety is minimized and everything happening around us is lost for the moment. We can knit many items using a basic stitch; therefore, beginners need not worry about running out of simple patterns. The challenge of attempting something new by using more complicated stitches can happen early or later in a knitter's career.

I have known knitters who have been creatively active their whole lives by using the same stocking stitch, garter stitch or seed stitch in different projects. Being ready to learn something new and to branch out into different levels of design, colour, pattern, and format does take courage and a willingness to leave a very secure comfort zone. Trial and error are huge parts of any adventure into the unknown, but the worst that can happen in knitting is that we rip out the entire project and begin again.

"I will even make a road through the wilderness and rivers in the desert." (NRSV) How reassuring is this promise when a knitter bumps up against a seemingly impossible situation? All is not lost but relaxing into the moment ensures that the hope of creating a new thing out of a mistake is empowering.

Seven

James 2:14 (NRSV)

"What good is it, my brothers and sisters, if you say you have faith but do not have works? Can faith save you?" (NRSV)

We hear of family violence almost daily in the media. Behavioural standards have changed along with family configurations. Many families are confused about what is right and about what is expected in respectful and loving relationships. Of necessity, havens for the victims of family violence have opened all over the world. Gifts of clothing, bedding and toiletries can boost the living requirements of affected families and are readily offered in most places. We can pray with them and for them, but displaced individuals need something more tangible to help them develop their faith.

Community kitchens provide a communal learning environment where trained leaders teach families how to purchase food items in bulk at the lowest cost. Not only do they learn to cook together, but how to share large quantities of food, making sure that there is enough food for one week.

While observing the children who accompany their parents to these lessons, it is not difficult to pick up on behavioural traits. Children are demoralized at the breakup of their families, and while some know that this is not of their own doing, others assume the blame.

Knowing of my love of knitting, a social worker asked if I would knit some dolls with their own drawstring pouches as this had been a successful project in another venue. She told me that many children do not want to talk about their situations but will give their worries to the dolls and will place their worries in these pouches, putting them under their pillows where the worries will dissipate overnight.

The request came with a pattern and I now had a reason to use my small balls of leftover wool. I knit worry dolls for teenage boys, too, as many ask for their own.

This indeed, is faith accompanied by action.

Having met many of these children, it is not difficult to incorporate prayer into every living stitch. I start knitting the doll's feet, work my way up the legs to the body, then the head, as I remember individual children's needs. As I use up the colours, I am pleasantly amazed at the end results. Each one is different as its own personality evolves during the process. The drawstring bag usually matches the colour combination of the clothing to avoid picking up the wrong piece in the communal area.

I also knit smaller dolls, all in one piece, with stitches to define the arms and the legs. These dolls are often included in the parcels of pneumonia prevention vests and preemie baby hats that are mailed to India and Africa. While knitting these smaller dolls, I enjoy listening to tranquil music, enabling me to delve deeply into my inner reserves and pray with compassion for the newer generation in these beleaguered countries. Who knows, perhaps they will have greater perseverance and moral strength to make significant changes in the lives of their own people.

> *"Faith, by itself, if it has no works, is dead."*
> *James 2:17(NRSV)*

My prayer is that God's love will enter the children's hearts, minds, and souls to give them the guidance and the knowledge to make a difference. My friends, who have attended church services in Malawi, have told me that our worship is embarrassingly weak compared to the theological commitment in a sanctuary filled to overflowing with people raising their beautiful voices in praise and adoration. Many families walk for hours to be there. Such heartfelt love cannot go unnoticed by God.

Eight

Isaiah 43:1(NRSV)

"But now thus says the Lord, he who created you, O Jacob, He who formed you, O Israel: Do not fear, for I have redeemed you; I have called you by name, you are mine."

There you go! Once again God is letting you know that He is waiting for you. No time is more important or more precious than the present. Nothing is more important than today. Stop whatever you are doing and claim your place with God now. Use whatever it takes for you to "be still and know that I am God."

I have suffered from little physical pain in my life, but for those who live with chronic pain you can use God's power to shift your focus away from the pain. No one deserves pain. Isaiah continues, "When you pass through the waters, I will be with you; and through the rivers, they shall not overflow you. When you walk through the fire, you shall not be burned, nor shall the flame scorch you."

Relax in your favourite chair. Have a cup of tea in your prettiest cup. Play some soothing Mozart and pick up your knitting needles. If you like, memorize the first two verses of Isaiah ch43 and repeat these as rhythmically as you can while you are moving stitches from one needle to another. You will be amazed at how calm you feel; rejoice in the everlasting promise of God.

Pleasantly, whatever you have on your needles, will have progressed almost unnoticed as you work through this exercise.

A distant relative of mine, Heather, suffered from the pain of rheumatoid arthritis for many years. Her hobby was collecting and creating miniatures. She built authentic creations of homesteading history, researching details and dates while discovering stories of local battles and important events. When she retired, she applied to the local education authorities, asking for permission to visit schools as an itinerant historian, taking her models with her.

She, and her craft, became a much-anticipated addition to the curriculum as students learned appreciatively from this visual aid.

* * *

Heather's arthritic pain increased as she aged, and she was afraid that she could no longer continue to do what she enjoyed.

Years earlier, she and her mother were local celebrities for their knitting and crocheting skills. Later, Heather found that despite her pain and disability, she was still able to hold and work with her knitting needles. Before packing up her tiny miniatures to visit a school, she relaxed in her rocking chair to knit a few rows of a shawl or a dishcloth. She realized that her pain had subsided enough to allow her to drive to her next appointment.

Heather probably did not realize that she had an inner spirituality where God was reaching into her pain threshold. She only knew that knitting worked.

Nine

John 19:23b (NRSV)

"now the tunic was seamless, woven in one piece from the top."

The painting, *Madonna Knitting*, by Bertram von Minden, shows Mary knitting a tunic on four needles and making it without a seam.

Before the crucifixion, the soldiers tried to rip Jesus' clothing off him, but the garment could not be torn. As they were unable to take and share the cloth, they decided to draw lots to see who should claim the garment. In verse 25 it says, "standing near the cross of Jesus, was his mother." I think it would make a wonderful story if we knew what Mary was thinking about this garment, which she purportedly made herself. In the painting, as she is knitting (in pink), Jesus was still a toddler lying at her feet. She looks so at peace and I imagine that Mary felt the same tranquility from knitting that most other knitters find.

Knitting on four double-pointed needles or on a circular needle is called knitting in the round. This eliminates the need for a seam. My first effort at knitting socks for my dad was on four double-pointed needles. This was an easy way to begin because the socks were in a plain knit stitch. There was no need to purl any stitches as this happens automatically in the round, except when knitting the cuff. Circular needles are needles with points at both ends and a length of plastic cable in the middle.

I wish those had been invented when I was in school, as I would frequently drop one needle onto the floor. This made the teacher angry and each time a classmate dropped a needle, our teacher, armed with a wooden ruler, would march around the room to wrap us across the knuckles because of our carelessness. I was unable to understand this action as the painful reaction caused us to be less careful and the needle would drop again.

* * *

I am going to paraphrase Hebrews 12:5&6 to suit my story.

> "And you have forgotten the exhortation which
> speaks to you as to *students*: *Students*, do not despise
> the chastening of the *teacher* nor be discouraged when
> you are rebuked by *her*, for whom the *teacher* loves
> she chastens and scourges every *student* she receives.
> Now no chastening seems to be joyful for the present
> but painful nevertheless, afterward it yields the
> peaceable fruit of righteousness to those who have
> been trained by it."

Many years later I realized that I was not being punished; I was being trained to become more careful.

A marker is one of the requirements of knitting in the round to indicate the beginning of each round. This eliminates confusion and avoids the possibility of having gone too far. This marker helps when we are knitting mindfully; trying to focus on our spiritual awareness. Knitting mindfully can become quite absorbing as it helps us focus on God for complete peace. There are many distractions in our everyday lives that make it difficult to maintain focus. The onus is on ourselves to bring us back into a centering position when we can shut everything out and just be.

The repetitive movement of transferring stitches from one needle to another creates a habit that moves us from the mundane to the spiritual. This is not always easy and often requires the use of an outside force. I like to use all my senses, and one of my favourite olfactory sensations is the smell of rosemary. I normally have a small dish in my kitchen. Though it does not grow well in my part of the world, I have a photograph of a rosemary hedge that was growing along a footpath to a beach in Southern California. If I look at this picture while handling the leaves of my rosemary plant, I become absorbed by its scent, enabling me to fully relax.

An act that is so simple but is another method that is often taken for granted.

Ten

Ephesians 3:17 – 19 (NRSV)

"that Christ may dwell in your hearts through faith, as you are being rooted and grounded in love. I pray that you may have the power to comprehend, with all the saints, what is the breadth and length and height and depth and to know the love of Christ that surpasses knowledge, so that you may be filled with all the fullness of God."

For individuals it is humanly unimaginable to comprehend the fullest dimensions of God's love for us. In our deepest grief, it is so hard to gain that knowledge, enough to believe that we may be filled with all the fullness of God. How can this be? We are mortal with all our human frailties, so how can this be? When we are rooted and grounded in love then the possibilities are endless. We must believe.

Isaiah 30:15 says,
"In repentance and rest is your salvation,
in quietness and trust is your strength."

I often return to my gratitude corner in repentance of many of my human failings.

K3, P3, I have failed to reach out to a friend suffering from the loss of a spouse.

K3, P3, I have been less than compassionate when a colleague suffers as a result of his own doing.

K3, P3, I have ignored a family member who has been silently in need.

K3, P3, I have not heeded your call to place me in yet another leadership role.

As I rest in God's salvation and forgiveness, I mentally mark the time when I can concentrate on these matters and make restitution.

K3, P3, I continue in solitude and silence as I gain strength to right all the wrongs which I have confessed.

K3, P3, K3, P3, the prayer shawl grows as I decide to whom I should give this special offering.

Because a prayer shawl is simple to knit, it is a perfect project to work on when those spare moments appear. I knit my shawls using a size 7 or 8 knitting needle and I cast on 63 stitches. As I knit in a pattern of knit 3, purl 3, the alternate row begins the same way, forming a delicate pattern on the finished article. I make my shawls in various lengths as some fit gently over the shoulders and around the back of the neck, while others are longer and can be wrapped around for extra warmth. For the longer shawls, three 6 oz (170 gm) balls of wool are required for a finished length of 60 inches. You can knit a shawl at any desired length depending on the amount of wool available; it is good to experiment with different textures and colours of wool. You can also finish the shawl with a knotted fringe.

Silently, and with gentle assurance, God continually makes His love known to me, but often I do not grasp the significance of these moments until later.

It seems like a coincidence that, after I confess my failure to reach out to a hurting friend, another friend calls me to ask for company on a visit to the same friend. Together we experience the love which God shares abundantly, making all of us feel so much better.

When I have baked too many muffins for my family, I wrap the extra few and drive to visit a lonely, elderly couple who are thrilled by my surprise visit. This exchange lifts their dragging spirits and I always come away with feeling so much richer.

My belief is that due to God's love for me I, in my busyness, can find that little gift of time to continue knitting as I remember to intercede in prayer for those less fortunate than myself. In my ability to understand the fullness of God's love for me, the assurance of pardon is so freely given and so gratefully accepted.

This is being filled with the fullness of God.

Eleven

Psalm 34:18 (NRSV)

"The Lord is near to the broken hearted
and saves the crushed in spirit."

Hearts are broken in so many ways and for so many reasons. It is impossible to understand someone else's heartache despite being empathetic to the situation. The depth of a broken heart is personal. A person in such emotional pain finds it difficult to comprehend the closeness of a compassionate God.

God has many ways of coming close to those whose hearts are broken and in need of repair. Those ways are usually through caring friends who are open to the nudges of a faithful God.

I can recall two stories as I delve into my memory bank and both relate to beautiful residents of senior care centres. As the population continues to age, many more people find care and comfort in such settings. However, because of the increasing number of residents combined with the decreasing number of caregivers, many of these seniors are left alone much of the time.

These are people who have led busy and useful lives and who do not respond well to being inactive and non-productive. This is one form of a broken heart. Someone saddened by the lack of ability and inclination to continue a fruitful existence.

My niece, Hazel, volunteered her time in one such facility but came away disappointed at the end of each visit as she was unable to elicit any kind of reaction from elderly white-haired Madge. As she attempted to find something to interest Madge, Hazel asked Madge's family about her interests in her earlier life. Her son mentioned that Madge's passion had been floral arrangements, but that she had been unable to work with her hands in recent years. On her next shift, Hazel brought floral wires, an oasis, some floral tape, and a few flowers.

Immediately, Madge's eyes opened wide and she smiled broadly as she began to loosen up her fingers to begin her craft. All those present shed a few tears.

"The Lord is near to the broken hearted
and saves the crushed in spirit."
Psalm 34:18

In another senior care centre, some members of the local phil-
harmonic society performed in a beautiful atrium. On one visit,
as the staff wheeled some residents along in their wheelchairs, no
one could persuade Archie to join them. He rarely spoke, but he
let the staff know that he refused and was determined to stay in
his room. One sympathetic chaplain felt that this outing might
be good for Archie, so she gently insisted on accompanying him.
After a while, Archie's hands were beating time to the music and
his eyes were fixed on the conductor. In a surprise move, Archie
stood up from his wheelchair, walked across the floor, and took
the baton from the conductor. The staff cried tears of disbelief as
Archie continued to conduct the orchestra.

Knitting, as well as any craft, hobby, or passion provides a link to the forgotten fruitful and meaningful life of yesteryear; memories that should not be allowed to go to waste.

"The Lord saves such as have a contrite spirit" is the second part of the scriptural quote. One dictionary describes contrite as "sorrowing for sin" (Oxford) while another (Collins) says "guilty and regretful."

Both Madge and Archie were saved from the torment of a wasted skill, whether they had any reason to have contrite spirits.

$Twelve$

Philippians 4:10, 13 (NRSV)

"Rejoice in the Lord greatly that now at last you have revived your
concern for me but had no opportunity to show it.
I can do all things through Him who strengthens me."

How often do we have concern for someone, but have difficulty showing that concern? We allow opportunities to slip past, thinking that there will be another time and perhaps another chance. What is the reticence that allows us to be so afraid of exposing ourselves to a failed attempt that we dishonour God by neglecting the needs of others?

For many years I convened a Conversation and Crafts group in the church that I attend. The participants were senior ladies who had left their home country in widowhood to be closer to family in their declining years. All were knitters of long- standing. The common bond was their love of yarn and needles and whatever could be produced by their hard work. These ladies were from different countries and spoke different languages, but as they came to know one another and became familiar with similar experiences, they told their stories, and we all learned a great deal.

As Jenny showed us how tatting was done, she reminisced of her early days in Nova Scotia as a district nurse. She told us of having to accompany the local doctor to a remote rural home where a little boy was suffering from scarlet fever. The child needed constant attention, so Jenny had to stay to nurse him until the doctor returned some days later. In her quiet moments, Jenny knitted and tatted to pass the time.

Bertha crocheted her way through many tablecloths and table runners as she waited for her husband to return from sea. He did not return from his final trip leaving Bertha to bring up her newly born daughter alone. She was in an unfamiliar city where she did not know anyone. The other residents of the Seaman's Mission Hostel were sorry for Bertha, as some had suffered from the same tragedy and were able to share their concerns. As Bertha had become a widow, she could no longer stay in the hostel and she returned to her family.

Maria had lived through the war years in Holland. While knitting furiously she spoke of the unbelievable injustices she had observed during that time. She shared many experiences with Olive, who had lived through the same experiences in England. They related stories of women and children in underground bunkers, sharing food rations as they listened for another bomb to drop.

The common thread through all these stories is that knitting was a way of life back then. The act of knitting rooted these ladies into their spirituality and their faith in God. Often in their forced isolation, they sang hymns and prayed to help ease their fears and discomfort. In the end, new sweaters, socks, scarves, and blankets were completed as the product of time well spent during the war years.

In this same group of crafters, a woman dropped in to see if she could sit amongst us. She had knitted in the past, but because of cobalt therapy she had lost much of the power in her fingers. She became engrossed in the handiwork of others and resolved to overcome her disability. With much patient encouragement from her new friends, she slowly increased her ability to the point where she was knitting small items on small needles. Craft activities result in tangible, useful products that can enhance one's self-esteem.

"I can do all things through Him who strengthens me."

Thirteen

Jeremiah29:13,14 (NRSV)

"'If you seek me with all your heart,
I will let you find me,' says the Lord."

This passage of scripture is familiar to me, but I have failed to realize that the importance of each word is filtered by skimming over it in its familiarity. The Lord says, "If you seek me"—not a scant look or a request in passing—but "with all your heart," blocking out all other distractions with passion and pleading, then "I will let you find me." God will let me find Him! It is almost like playing hide-and-seek with a child when you let them find you as you want to bring them the joy. This is the same with God. It is hard for me to believe that in the many times I have read this passage, yet I have never noticed that God would let me find Him if I were to seek Him with all my heart.

The coincidence of reading this passage happened recently to me. I usually end my prayers of requests and intercessions with, "not my will but yours, God, and in your time not mine." That day my request was spontaneous, specific, time-sensitive, and almost groveling, but God's response was also spontaneous, specific, and time-sensitive. I still marvel at the sequence of events in this true story.

My 18-year-old granddaughter had bought a second-hand graduation gown. She was delighted with her purchase but asked if I would alter it as it was too large for her.

Although I had not seen the gown, I was happy to alter it to suit her expectations. She waited many weeks before she brought the dress to me, so I had little time to work on the alterations. As I was shown this beautifully elegant dress, I noticed a bodice of sequins, stones, and lace all intertwined. I hoped that I could justify my grand-daughter's confidence in my capability. She had failed to inform me that the dress was a size 10 and she needed it to be a size 00!

Like knitting, I find that working with fabric is just as relaxing without the repetition. The texture of fabric varies considerably and the tactile effects of working with cotton, satin, silk, and linen encourages me to be creative. When I thought that I had finished transforming the dress, my granddaughter decided that I had not tightened the bodice enough and asked me to take it in another inch on either side of the zipper. I felt uncomfortable with the degree of difficulty as I sought to comply with this request. With much trepidation, I was sure that I had ruined the dress by the time it was ready for the graduation ball. Another complication was that the dress had seven layers of skirt and was seven inches too long.

* * *

I gave up! The day before graduation, I visited every dress shop in the area, and none of whom had a size 00 in stock. I called every dressmaker I knew, who, at this time were busy with other graduation alterations. I felt deflated and desperate.

In the heat of a lovely summer day with the birds singing joyfully, I knelt on my deck and pleaded with God. "This has to work, Lord. You and I need to work together to make this a success." That was the essence of a much longer prayer, which I prayed with passion and determination.

I felt encouraged after a while and I went to my sewing room to rip out the zipper in one last attempt. Miraculously, the line of sequins and beads fell into place as I hand-stitched the final neckline. Two of the skirt layers were hemmed, but the others were easy to trim as my granddaughter stood on a coffee table circling as I cut the layers. This was the night before graduation!

God let me find Him as we worked together on a seemingly impossible venture.

Fourteen

John 14:27 (NRSV)

"Peace is what I leave with you; it is my own peace that I give you. I do not give it as the world does. Do not be worried and upset; do not be afraid."

This is such a comforting verse of scripture and can be called upon in so many different circumstances. The usual place to hear this passage is during a funeral or a memorial service. When this verse stands on its own, it is difficult to digest during such an emotional time, so some inferences may be missed. Jesus is giving away peace and is leaving it with us. A peace that belongs to Him alone and He is generously offering it for the taking.

To emphasize the difference in the peace which He is giving, Jesus clarifies that His peace is not one that comes from the world. In times of grief, a sense of peace can come from wonderful friends and well-meaning neighbours who bring a casserole, send a card, give us flowers, or make a sympathetic phone call which is always welcome and accepted with deep gratitude. Yes, they offer a sense of peace, but Jesus wants us to know that He wants to shower us in a deeper and longer-lasting spiritual peace which will wipe away all worry and fear.

In this wonderful world of God's immaculate creation, there are some individuals who embrace this type of peace as a matter of reality. Most Indigenous communities come to mind, but my thoughts are drawn to the communities in the Outer Hebrides of Scotland a generation ago.

A major part of the crofting life in these Western Isles of Scotland was undertaken by women who were hardened to the wild, windy, wet weather familiar to the region. They raised sheep for the beautifully soft wool that was in demand throughout the world. They would sheer the sheep; card the wool, then spin the wool before winding it into skeins that are required for knitting. All of this took place as part of their organized, formatted daily routine through the seasons despite the weather patterns. These women worked together in their small communities and were often related to one another. Every step of their day happened in a peaceful manner, moving from one task to another while waltzing their way throughout their routines. During their spinning process, they sang in time to the turn of the wheel, but they often shared stories. This is where the term "spinning a yarn" comes from.

One of the hardest tasks these women undertook was carrying peat from the peat bogs to their homes for their fires. Able men would cut the peat into bricks and would lay them to dry. The women collected the bricks in creels, which were large panniers carried on their backs, but were supported by leather straps around their foreheads. As they trundled back to their cottages, they spent their walking time chatting and singing as they went.

In reminiscing over the lifestyles of long ago, I sense that they were much more aware of the presence of God in their lives. Today it is good to remember to slow down and enjoy the everyday realities that enrich our souls.

Fifteen

Psalm 23 (NRSV)

"The Lord is my shepherd; I shall not want."

It is so fitting for knitters to know that God is our personal shepherd since sheep are the source of the wool that we lovingly create into a finished article.

I grew up on a general-purpose farm where we milked cattle, herded sheep, raised pigs, farmed poultry, and grew grain and root crops. Many men were employed to cover all these disciplines, and each was an expert in his own field.

My dad, a dairyman, knew everything about cows and each of his cows had a name. He kept records about when each cow was due to calf, how much milk production was produced annually, and totalled the amount of butter fat and cream in the content. He also told me and my brothers to stay out of the sterile dairy where the fresh milk was cooled, but one of the boys dared to defy this law and approached the milk cooler to enjoy a drink of cold milk as it rippled down from the tank. Unfortunately, his lips stuck to the ice-cold metal, causing much distress and a stern warning against a repeat performance.

Once a year, it was necessary to herd the sheep to a specific location and guide them through a trough of liquid strong disinfectant. This would kill any maggots in their wool prior to the shearing process. The shepherd's wife was an avid knitter, so while all this outside work was being done, she brought her stool and her knitting bag to ply her craft while she watched. As she was part of the annual process—that kept her husband away for long hours—she was given a sense of peace.

Harvest time was one of my favourite seasons on the farm. Each October, our schools were closed for a week so that we could provide much of the paid labour for potato gathering. We began early in the morning, working our way along the rows by lifting the potatoes turned over by a tractor blade. We had snack breaks and a lunch break, but by the end of every day we were very tired. As we anticipated and received our payment at the end of that week, we knew that all the hardship was worthwhile.

In my day, haymaking was an art before the introduction of heavy machinery. The long grass was cut and left to dry before being built into stacks. As the men tossed the hay with the pitchforks, the mice scrambled, and dust blew into the men's eyes. After such work, they became very hungry and thirsty. My mother, and other farm wives, baked scones and pan scones and filled flasks of tea that were delivered to the hayfield in baskets for a mid-afternoon snack. This was an especially happy time of fellowship, and yes, knitting accompanied the ladies to the field where they shared their news and waited till the baked goodies were finished before returning home.

God never makes mistakes and everything that takes place is always with a reason and for a purpose. In the busyness of life, it is essential for our well-being to slow down and take time to just be still, to assess our feelings which we are guilty of storing deep within ourselves. God sees that inner space and if we relax with intention, He will gently help us until we are aware that God truly is waiting for us in the inner sanctuary of our souls.

CPSIA information can be obtained
at www.ICGtesting.com
Printed in the USA
BVHW061924070721
611295BV00021B/272